Revolutionary Portraits  **William Blake**

William Blake
THE SCOURGE OF TYRANTS

Judy Cox

REVOLUTIONARY PORTRAIT 6

William Blake: the scourge of tyrants by Judy Cox

Published in 2004 by

REDWORDS

1 Bloomsbury Street, London WC1B 3QE

www.redwords.org.uk

ISBN: 1 872208 21 5

Design and production: Roger Huddle and Hannah Dee
Printed by Cambridge Printing, Cambridge

Redwords is linked to Bookmarks the socialist bookshop
www.bookmarks.uk.com

Etching of Blake taken from a portrait by Thomas Phillipps

This book is in the series **Revolutionary Portraits** from Redwords. The unifying theme in this eclectic collection is the relationship between individual artists and larger historical forces, how each influences and shapes the other. All of the books in this series aim to lead us back to these works of art and music with new eyes and ears, and a deeper understanding of how art can raise the human spirit.

Redwords is a publishing collective specialising in art, history and literature from a socialist perspective.
We are linked to Bookmarks, the socialist bookshop.

Reader! *[Lover]* of books! *[Lover]* of heaven,
And of that God from whom *[all books are given,]*
Who in mysterious Sinais awful cave
To Man the wond'rous art of writing gave,
Again he speaks in thunder and in fire!
Thunder of Thought, & flames of fierce desire:
Even from the depths of Hell his voice I hear,
Within the unfathomd caverns of my Ear.
Therefore I print; nor vain my types shall be:
Heaven, Earth & Hell, henceforth shall live in harmony

William Blake, *Jerusalem: The Emanation of The Giant Albion,* 1804

CONTENTS

Revolution: the master theme of the epoch[1]

William Blake wrote some of the most original and enduringly popular poems of the English language. The poem 'Jerusalem' was set to music by Charles Parry in 1916. It became known as 'Jerusalem' when Parry conducted it in 1918 at a concert for the votes for women campaign. It has become an unofficial national anthem. It is sung by the respectable ladies of middle England in the Women's Institute. It ranks alongside 'Land of Hope and Glory' in the hearts of the Tory party, while New Labour considers it to be a politically acceptable alternative to the too subversive 'Red Flag'. His children's poems such as 'Tyger' are still recited by school kids.

Why should a poet and artist approved of by such pillars of the establishment be interesting to socialists? Because this obscure, poverty-stricken artisan created some of the most powerful images of revolutionary energy and human liberation that have ever been produced. His was the voice that spoke out for the enslaved and abandoned and was raised in never-ending accusation against an unjust world of exploitation.

William Blake attracted little attention during his lifetime, but has subsequently become the focus of many worthy literary studies. Yet he remains a curiously obscure figure, part of many traditions and at the same time an original. One Blake biographer, the Marxist historian E P Thompson, lists the scholarly volumes that describe Blake, 'the neo-platonist, the mason and illuminist, the profound initiate in hermetic learning, the proto-Marxist, the euhemist, the Druid'.[2] However, the further back we go, the closer we get to the living Blake, the more clear the real William Blake becomes. Blake's first biographer, Alexander Gilchrist, wrote in 1863 of his eccentricity, genius and robust 'Jacobinical' convictions.

Blake was a Jacobin. He looked forward to the possibilities created by the French Revolution. But he also looked backwards, and sought guidance from the Bible. He absorbed and reinterpreted the dissenting traditions he inherited from the English Revolution of the 1640s, when Christianity was the language of political debate. The possibility of overthrowing tyrants, of levelling the rich and of creating a heaven on earth were all part of Blake's mental landscape. His Everlasting Gospel was a gospel of rebellion against the tyrannical god of the Old Testament, and all state religion and government. But it was a contradictory inheritance. It incorporated a revolution that turned the world upside down. It also involved the experience of defeat that saw the monarchy restored to the throne and masses sink back in their place.

It was not only the revolutions of the past that fired Blake's imagination. Revolt framed Blake's life and his art. Between 1760, just after Blake was born, and 1815, just before Blake died, England was obsessed by revolutions, the great social convulsions which gave birth to the modern world. There were political revolutions and attempted revolutions in America (1775-82), in Geneva (1782), in Holland (1794) in Poland (1794), in Ireland (1798) and in Naples (1799) and the Great French Revolution which began in 1789. Revolution was the central social experience of these years. The French Revolution shattered the idea that change could be best achieved constitutionally. Thousands of English men and women began to organise to claim their own right to liberty and equality. Not surprisingly the process of revolution features directly in many literary works of the era. These included William Blake's 'America', Robert Southey's 'Thalaba the Destroyer', Lord Byron's 'Corsair', Shelley's 'Revolt of Islam' and John Keats's 'Hyperion'.

The revolutions were met with war and imperialism. The wars against France of 1793-1815 cost more British dead, proportional to the population, than the First World War.[3] In protest against these wars, Blake wrote:

'The strongest poison ever known
Came from Caesar's laurel crown.
Nought can deform the Human Race
Like to the Armour's iron brace'.[4]

The British clash with Napoleon's armies became a 'world war'. These two imperialist nations were battling for the right to exploit the non-European globe. At least 50,000

British lives were lost in the struggle for control of the West Indies.[5] Between 1795 and 1805 the British Empire was established, with the effective annexation of the Indian sub-continent from Ceylon to the Himalayas. These changes also found their artistic expression in the work of the romantic poets: 'If there is one theme which binds, William Blake (whom contemporaries barely knew) to Scott and Byron (by whom they were dazzled): that theme is empire and its imagined overthrow, which is both longed for and dreaded'.[6]

Another revolution, this time an economic one, was intimately linked with the political revolutions. Before Blake was born, Britain was a country whose world trade was founded in the village. During Blake's lifetime, production moved to the factory. This Industrial Revolution transformed how men and women produced and reproduced their lives. It also transformed how they saw themselves and their world. So long as men were tied to the land and lived in villages, they believed their jobs were a gift from a superior being – either God, or the local lord. The move to factory production transformed the labourer from a skilled craftsman who worked with his hands into a waged worker with nothing to offer but his hands. An economic slump was different from a drought or flood. Unemployment was caused not by not God or nature but by the master, the factory owner, the boss. The upheaval of the revolutions 'forced men in the long run to seek their destiny, and to find their station, not in the hand of God, but in their own hands'.[7] People were beginning to shake off both natural and supernatural powers and face their destiny. This painful process is just visible in the poetry of William Blake.

During Blake's lifetime these upheavals led to an explosion of hope that ordinary men and women could build a society based on universal equality. This hope affected every aspect of life. After the French Revolution, philosopher Isaac D'Israeli wrote that 'within the present century a great Revolution was effected in the human mind. Philosophers ceased to be isolated. It is but of late that the people have been taught to read, and still later, that they have learned to think'.[8] The whole range of political debates were fought out through the written word. In 1790 Edmund Burke wrote *Reflections on the Revolution in France*, in which he condemned the 'swinish multitude', the revolutionary masses. He was countered by Mary Wollstonecraft's *A Vindication of the Rights of Man* (her *A Vindication of the Rights of Woman* came later) and Thomas Paine's hugely popular *Rights of Man*. Both radicals and reactionaries wrote novels to promote their political views. Art was a weapon of both right and left, its language was a political language. When the British state clamped down on radicals, it targeted writers and publishers as well agitators and organisers.

William Pitt's government unleashed a reign of terror against British radicals in 1792. His war against ordinary people went on for much longer. More people were executed for crimes against property in England during these years than were executed during the Terror in France. Shelley called this period the 'age of despair', but radical ideas were never crushed completely. They survived in the organisations of the labouring class, they survived in the pages of Thomas Paine's *Rights of Man*, which sold a million copies, and they survived in the poetry which expressed the experience of revolution and counter-revolution, as Blake's did.

He had a unique perspective among the poets. He was rooted in the artisan community of London, he inhabited workshops, not drawing rooms. He did not observe the social upheavals of the era – he lived them, as a craftsman battling against mechanisation, a freethinker facing the standardisation of art and as a fiercely independent mind forced to depend on rich patrons. Karl Marx's exasperated mother once wrote to him, 'Never has one man written so much about Capital, and enjoyed so little of it.' No one understood better than Blake the devastating impact of the free market on the artisans, yet no one suffered more from the lack of a market for their own work.

Blake's vision was extraordinary. He could embrace the universe and a flea, grand cosmic schemes and a beggar child living on a London street. He used the language of religious dissent, but he described the aspirations and defeats of the revolutionary era he experienced. He constructed mythical prophecies but also prophesied the development of social forces which would come to dominate the 19th and 20th centuries. As Jacob Bronowski wrote, 'Through all his poems, there sound the iron footsteps of the modern age: war, oppression, the machine, poverty and the loss of personality. This is the prophetic power of Blake: that he felt the coming disasters of war, empire and industry in his bloodstream, long before politicians and economists shivered at their shadows'.[9] Blake's reputation has grown through the decades since his death because his premonitions have become real.

Blake wanted to show in art the 'portion of eternity' he saw in his imagination. His great achievement was to develop the technical and artistic capability to communicate his visions. But Blake's visionary world did not exist in isolation from his physical world. The industrial innovations of the late 18th century, the spinning jenny, coke burning, steams engines, all appear in Blake's poems. The political hopes raised in the revolutions of America and France shine through in some of his prophetic books. The question also raised, that of identifying the force capable of winning universal rights and liberating the masses from poverty, haunts Blake's mystical world. His characters strive for freedom but are constantly defeated. They cannot rationalise and theorise their way to freedom. Their plight parallels that of the radical intellectuals who lacked the means to realise their ideals. For all his mysticism and complexity, Blake speaks to those who condemn the oppression he so despised and strive for the human liberation he so desired.

Blakean energy and joyous form: *Glad Day*, c1794, British Museum

Why was I born with a different face?
Why was I not born like the rest of my race?

When Blake was born at 7.45pm on Monday 28 November 1757, his parents James and Catherine already had two sons, James and John. James and Catherine Blake were tradespeople, comfortable but not rich. They ran a hosiery and haberdashery business on Golden Square, off Broad Street, central London. When he grew up, Blake's brother James took over the family business. The Blake family were part of a dissenting tradition widespread among London's traders and artisans. The dissenters were never deferential to their earthly superiors. They brought their children up to believe as they did. James junior was as dutiful in belief as he was in business. He would 'talk Swedenborg', the founder of a dissenting sect, well into his middle age.[10] William Blake took the dissenters' faith in the Bible to his heart and it stayed there all his life. So did the dissenters' hatred of authority and hierarchy.

Peter Ackroyd gives a very evocative description of young William's London, then still more medieval than modern. The heads of executed criminals still rotted on poles above Temple Bar. There were regular riots, some for bread, some for 'Wilkes and Liberty'. Oxford Street and its surrounding lanes were muddy, stinking and dangerous pathways. The Blake family home backed onto a parish workhouse, itself built on a burial ground. The smell from both was appalling. The sufferings of the workhouse inmates must have had an impact on the imaginative young William.

William Blake wrote and read poetry, including Milton's 'Paradise Lost', when he was a young child. He drew, and visited art galleries. His family hung his drawings up around their home. He was a solitary child who loved wandering alone around the London streets and across the open fields off Tottenham Court Road. He would have known the London pubs and fairs, the brick kilns and butchers, the pickpockets and the prostitutes.[11] Blake's London was bloated with refugees from rural misery. The desperation bred in the towns can be imagined from some raw statistics: in the year Blake was born England consumed 8 million gallons of gin – a gallon for every man, woman and child in the country.

William was sent to Pars drawing school, where he first became fascinated by the old masters, Michelangelo and Raphael and the engravings of Albrecht Dürer. But Blake did not go to study art at the Royal Academy School. He could not monopolise his parents' wealth at the expense of his brothers and younger sister. Instead, he became apprenticed to an engraver. One story from these years concerned William Ryland, a fashionable and expensive engraver. William was seeking an apprenticeship. When he was taken to meet this prospective master, he said to his Dad, 'I do not like the man's face: it looks as if he will live to be hanged.' Ryland was indeed the last man hanged at Tyburn, some 12 years later. However, this precocious insight did not prevent Blake befriending Thomas Wainewright some years later. Thomas Wainewright was also hanged, for being a poisoner.

Whether because of Blake junior's dislike of the man, or Blake senior's dislike of his high charges, William was apprenticed to a very different man in August 1772. James Basire, of Great Queen Street, Lincoln's Inn Fields, was steady and old-fashioned. The terms of the apprenticeship remained rooted in the medieval world. The 14 year old Blake promised not to fornicate or marry, not to game or dice, and not to haunt taverns or playhouses for the duration of his apprenticeship. On his side, Basire promised to teach him engraving and feed him and clothe him for the next seven years.

Both read the bible day & night
But thou readst black where I read white

Basire's style of art focused on outline and the correct depiction of form, in contrast to the construction of images through light and shade, the method preferred by artists like Titian and Rembrandt. Blake learnt to draw pure, flowing and 'flaming lines'. At Basire's Blake learnt to see the monumental dimensions of the 'human form divine', especially the nude human form, from ancient Greek art. William was sent to make sketches of the Gothic monuments in Westminster Abbey. This set his imagination on fire. He had to cope with cold, scaffolding and teasing schoolboys, but he still called the abbey, 'the radiant temple of God'. He never lost his deep love for Gothic art.

Blake felt the ancient Gothic was the pinnacle of Christian art. It blended with another great influence on his life, the Bible. Blake called himself an 'enthusiastic hope-fostered visionary'.[12] The dissenters believed that all truth could be found in the pages of the Bible, rather than in priestly, high-church interpretations of its texts. They believed all man-made institutions like the established church and state were tyrannical and Christ would free humanity from them. Only the authority of individual conscience should be recognised. Blake believed that Christ:

'Seventy Disciples sent
Against Religion & Government.'

Blake and his fellow dissenters were not just cranks on the margins of society. They formed a network of anti-establishment groups in chapels and taverns across their London. This was a space where experiments in democracy could be conducted free from the control of the gentry, the corrupt corporation, the monarchy.[13] As Blake wrote:

'The Church is cold,
But the Ale-house is healthy & pleasant and warm.'

In London in the 1780s and 1790s people were motivated to get involved and build their own systems. Blake's contemporaries 'joined different congregations and churches, fractured them through debate, created their own (just as Trotskyists would do generations later)'.[14] They believed in education and established hugely influential academies in places like Hoxton and Hackney. The dissenters' academies produced people of the intellectual stature of Thomas Paine, Mary Wollstonecraft, Robert Owen, William Hazlitt and John Keats.

Blake was deeply critical of religions which preached submission, for example, John Wesley's church which preached submission to the law. Writer Daniel Defoe caustically suggested that the Wesleyans wanted to reform the habits of the poor and nothing else. Blake understood as well as anyone how religion, even of the unsteepled, chapel variety, could be used to repress human pleasure, as his poem 'The Garden of Love' shows:

'I went to the Garden of Love,
And saw what I never had seen:
A Chapel was built in the midst,
Where I used to play on the green
And the gates of this Chapel were shut,
And "Thou shalt not" writ over the door;
So I turn'd to the Garden of Love
That so many sweet flowers bore;
And I saw it was filled with graves,
And tomb-stones where flowers should be;
And Priests in black gowns were walking their rounds,
And binding with briars my joys & desires.'

Blake knew some religions promised their compliant congregations pie in the sky when they die. He hated the priests who offered prayers to the hungry:

'They reduce Man to want, then give with pomp
   & ceremony:
The praise of Jehovah is chaunted from lips of
   hunger & thirst.'

The dissenters quoted the Bible and John Bunyan's *The Pilgrim's Progress*, they became Calvinists, Ranters, Diggers, Muggletonians and Ancient Deists. In their company Blake seems a lot less cranky and eccentric. As A L Morton points out, Blake was writing in a populist tradition.[15] Blake had his roots in the centuries-old dissenting tradition, where the difference between religious faith and political activism was always blurred. At the end of his life, in 'Jerusalem', Blake wrote, 'Are not Religion & Politics the Same Thing? Brotherhood is Religion.' This was not an abstract ideal of universal brotherhood. Blake's brothers were those who took up arms against tyranny.

During 1775, as Blake was learning his craft and his Bible, the American colonies revolted. The colonies were only allowed to trade with England, they could not manufacture their own products nor could they have a say in their own government. The American Revolution rapidly became a cause célèbre for English radicals. This was because of sympathy for their struggle against injustice. It was because the colonies were fighting for freedom and representation, exactly what the British radicals were campaigning for. The colonised established an exciting precedent in revolting against unpopular ministers, unpopular laws and, above all, God's unpopular representative on earth, King George III. Blake fully understood the implications of the revolt for the monarchy. Later, he wrote how, 'The King of England looking westwards, trembles at the vision.'

Like the American rebels, Blake was not prepared to simply accept his appointed station in life. When he finished his apprenticeship he didn't join the Stationers' Guild, which was the next step to becoming an engraver. Instead, prompted by a visit from an angel, he applied to join the Royal Academy of Arts. Blake was accepted by the academy, situated in the old Somerset House just off the Strand, in July 1779. He was to study engraving, to attend lectures and to draw. But one of the key lessons he learnt was that the academy prized conformity at the expense of creativity and innovation.

Improvement makes straight roads;
But the crooked roads are roads of genius

The very existence of the Royal Academy pointed to a growing specialisation in the arts. It was only during Blake's lifetime that painters achieved a status superior to that of artisans. The painters were jealous of their new-found position. In 1768 they split away from the Society of Artists, which the engraver William Howarth had held together, and formed the Royal Academy. Joshua Reynolds was its president. His priorities were stamped on the whole establishment. Reynolds believed that the purpose of the academy was to educate its pupils in the concept of 'ideal beauty' and 'intellectual dignity'. Cynics joked that the academy pursued perfect manners with more vigour than it pursued perfect beauty. Blake found the neoclassicism of the academy at odds with the Gothic style so central to his outlook. As one biographer put it, 'Blake preferred the rugged and the grand, while his teachers preferred the polished and the bland'.[16]

Blake's continuing reverence for Michelangelo and Raphael was testimony to his independence. They only came to be accepted as great masters during Blake's lifetime. At this time, Rubens and Titian would have been considered far superior artists. However, his insistence on following Michelangelo may have inhibited the development of Blake's own independent style. Michelangelo's art was linked with a whole renaissance in art and science. Blake was isolated from, and sometimes opposed to, the great innovations of his own world: 'Michelangelo had not laboured after the ancients. His drawings had been discoveries: the discovery of a single order, the machine, in man and in the world. Blake the craftsman was already at odds with the machine and knew of no other discovery to order his vision'.[17]

However, the conflict which developed between Blake and the academy was not really about artistic styles. It was a conflict of worldviews between the honest artisan and the polite gentlemen. Later Blake called Sir Joshua's teachers a 'gang of hired knaves'. He scribbled furious notes on the margins of a book by Reynolds. It is a typically Blakean rant against hypocrisy and pretensions:

Reynolds: I felt my ignorance and stood abashed.

Blake: A Liar he never was Abashed in his Life & never felt his Ignorance.

Reynolds: I consoled myself by remarking that these ready inventors, are extremely apt to acquiesce in imperfection.

Blake: Villainy a Lie.

Reynolds: But as mere enthusiasm will carry you but a little way…

Blake: Damn the Fool, Mere Enthusiasm is the All in All.'

Blake was not just protesting against genteel taste. He was protesting against art becoming nothing more than a marketable commodity and artists becoming tradesmen forced to sell their wares to survive. He felt the process by which art was 'transformed from a process in which the artists develops the self and humanises nature into a means to his mere physical existence'.[18] Blake was raging against the first signs of a process Marx described some years later: 'The bourgeoisie has stripped of its halo every occupation hitherto honoured and looked up to with reverent awe. It has converted the physician, the lawyer, the priest, the poet, the man of science, into its paid wage labourers'.[19]

Blake felt the neoclassicism imposed by the Academy was at one with its dry convention and commercialisation. Blake's dislike of the academy's classicism was 'of a piece with his social anger'.[20] He was contemptuous of way artisans were robbed of their living through new mechanised processes then patronised with offers of charity:

'The Enquiry in England is not whether a Man has Talents & Genius, But whether he is Passive & Polite & a Virtuous Ass & obedient to Noblemen's Opinions in Art & Science.
If he is, he is a Good Man. If Not, he must be Starved. Liberality! we want not Liberality. We want a Fair Price & Proportionate Value & a General Demand for Art.
This Whole Book was Written to Serve Political Purposes.'

Blake did, however, meet some good teachers at the academy. One was James Barry, a Professor of Painting and successful artist. He also met some very good friends among his fellow students. Thomas Stothard had been apprenticed to a silk weaver in Spitalfields. Later, under the patronage of Josiah Wedgwood, he became one of the most fashionable artists of his day. He introduced Blake to John Flaxman. Flaxman became the closest thing Blake had to a lifelong friend. There was not too much competition for this role, because Blake was too bewildering, too grumpy and too tactless to maintain many long friendships. Ironically, Flaxman was one of the most famous and influential sculptors of his time, but is now virtually unknown. Blake, his protégé, was utterly obscure in his own lifetime, but is now famous.

The friends were drawn together by shared interests. They all venerated Gothic art and were suspicious of neoclassicism. But their friendship was linked by more than their taste in art. Stothard, Flaxman and Blake were all committed political radicals.[21] They disliked the war with America, the repression in Ireland, the slave trade, and 'Old Corruption' (the English political establishment). Politics intruded directly on their lives. One day Stothard and Blake went on a sketching expedition to the River Medway. Soldiers suddenly appeared and arrested them as foreign spies. Members of the Royal Academy were fetched to vouch for them and they were released. The incident indicates the atmosphere in England during Blake's youth, the fear of invasion from without and subversion from within.

Energy is eternal delight

The England of Blake's youth was a land of riots. The combination of rising prices, heavier taxes and a hungry, angry population with no democratic representation proved highly volatile. Benjamin Franklin helped to draft the American Declaration of Independence but he lived in England from 1757 to 1774. He described how in 1769 alone England experienced 'riots about corn; riots about elections; riots about workhouses; riots of colliers; riots of weavers; riots of coalheavers; riots of sawyers; riots of sailors; riots of Wilkites, riots of government chairman, riots of smugglers'.[22] John Wilkes was a radical who was elected to, and expelled from, parliament and eventually became Alderman of London. He had some expertise in arousing the urban mob to protest for 'liberty' while keeping the demonstrators under control. There was also a tradition of groups associated with leading figures in the City of London stirring up riots to reinforce their campaigns.

In June 1780, 60,000 marched through London to

demand the repeal of the Catholic Relief Act. The marchers were stirred up by the gentlemen of the City, who wanted to create a political crisis in the hope of ending the war with America (it was proving bad for business). The London crowd was at first well disciplined, with respectable dissenting congregations out in force. But the law-abiding Protestants went home and their place on the streets was taken by rowdier types that made up the London mob. They had some political motivations and some mischievous ones. The arson attacks spread from Catholic houses to those of ministers, magistrates, judges and bishops and then to courts, prisons, the Bank of England and, rather opportunistically, to public houses. The Gordon Riot was under way.

The climax of the riot was the burning of Newgate jail and the freeing of the prisoners. The rioters included women and black people. Those they released were almost exclusively people with no property whose crimes were against property. Newgate was the symbol of the empire, the source of the repression which enforced the new means of exploitation. 'For the first time an international proletariat directly attacked the imperial ruling class at its major institutions, and so gave that class a serious fright'.[23] The revenge of the authorities was predictably bloody. Some 300 rioters were killed, with a further 62 condemned to death. Many young men of Blake's age were hanged for doing what he did.

For Blake was certainly among the head of the crowd which burned down Newgate. Was he there by accident or design? According to one report he was 'forced to go along in the very front rank' of the mob that went to Newgate. His friend George Cumberland was horrified by the rioters. Some have concluded that 'Blake, too, was a horrified witness of these outrages',[24] but there is no evidence of any horror on Blake's part. Cumberland's revulsion was not universal. Benjamin Franklin, for example, wrote about the burning of Chief Justice's house with some satisfaction: 'Thus, he who approved the burning of American houses, has had fire brought home to him'.[25]

Blake made contradictory engravings in the aftermath of the Gordon Riot. 'Albion Rose' is an image of exaltation, energy and liberation. It could express the unity and purpose of the mob. The lines which relate to the engraving are 'Albion rose from where he labour'd at the mill with slaves'. This relates directly to John Milton's 'Samson Agonistes', where Samson in one last heroic effect of revenge against his oppressors pulls their temple down on them. Others argue that this picture may be about Blake's freedom from his apprenticeship but it is a universal, glorious image.

In his wonderful study *Blake*: *Prophet Against Empire*, David Erdman writes that 'Albion Rose', or 'Glad Day', is Blake's representation of the English people doing their dance of insurrection. Erdman quotes political philosopher Edmund Burke describing the Gordon Riots as a time when 'wild and savage insurrection quitted the woods and prowled about our streets in the name of Reform'. Burke said it was a close-run thing as to whether it would be France or England that 'had the honour of leading up the death-dance of democratic revolution'. [26]

Lovely copulation, bliss on bliss

When Catherine Boucher met William Blake she recognised instantly that he was her future partner. She nearly fainted. Blake was still getting over his relationship with a girl who refused to be faithful to him, or to marry him. This was an era of sexual freedom but Blake wanted loyalty. Like Shakespeare's Romeo, Blake intended to moan about his lover but found a new and lovelier one. Catherine pitied his hurt and he loved her for her kindness.

He worked for a year as a professional engraver, often working as the junior artistic partner to his friend Thomas Stothard, to earn enough money for their marriage. It took place in August 1782. Catherine was from a poor family and signed the register with an X. They moved to a street near Leicester Square. Together they walked for hours to Blackheath, Dulwich and the ancient, picturesque town of Croydon.[27] They were parted for only a few days in 45 years of marriage. They worked together, comforted and entertained each other. The only serious row recorded occurred when Catherine fell out with Blake's beloved younger brother Robert and had to apologise to him.

Blake biographer Peter Ackroyd suggests that William Blake was a misogynist who hated 'what were then considered to be the "female virtues"'. Landscapes were associated with the female body and Blake hated landscapes too. Ackroyd also argues that the eroticism in Blake's work was abstract and theoretical, rather than drawn from experience. Yet everything about Blake's life and art suggests the contrary.

Wiliam seems to have enjoyed an exceptionally close and loving relationship with Catherine. He taught her to read and write and she helped him with his engravings. He leapt to the defence of women, literally in the case of one woman he saw being beaten by her husband in the street. Blake's defence was so vigorous that the woman's attacker 'recoiled and collapsed'. Blake's poems and pictures exude an unusual sympathy for abandoned women, prostitutes and working women. Blake treated sexuality as an important part of human existence and sought to free people from the guilt all too often linked to sexual pleasure.

In an astonishing poem, 'A Little Girl Lost', Blake describes a young girl who meets her lover 'Naked in the sunny beam's delight' and gets into trouble. The poem begins:

'Children of the future Age
Reading this indignant page,
Know that in a former time
Love! sweet Love! was thought a crime.'

Blake was an opponent of the censorship of desire and an advocate of sexual freedom and pleasure. Thus, in some extraordinary passages of poetry, Blake argues that sex should not just be about penetration:

'Embraces are Cominglings: from the Head,
     even to the Feet;
And not a pompous High Priest entering
     a secret Place.'

He was fiercely critical of those who 'suppose that Woman's

Love is Sin, and in consequence all the Loves and Graces with them are Sin'. Blake's 'Visions of the Daughters of Albion' centres on a passionate plea for sexual liberation. Oothoon, the heroine, imagines being with her lover:

> 'In happy copulation: if in evening mild, wearied
>   with work,
> Sit on a bank and draw the pleasures of this freeborn joy.
> The moment of desire! The moment of desire!
> The virgin
> That pines for man; shall awaken her womb to
>   enormous joys
> In the secret shadows of her chamber; the youth
>   shut up from
> The lustful joy shall forget to generate & create
>   an amorous image
> In the shadows of his curtains and in the folds of
>   his silent pillow.'

Blake was a fierce advocate of women's right to be free and to be fulfilled.

They accuse!

During the early 1780s William Blake was justifiably optimistic about his career. His commercial engravings were becoming just about profitable. Four of his pictures were exhibited at the Royal Academy in 1785. He had set up a print shop with his partner, James Parker, and bought a printing press to produce for commercial printing and his own illuminated books. The Blakes and the Parkers all lived upstairs in a house in Broad Street, with a studio also upstairs and a shop that Catherine ran downstairs.

Blake's social and intellectual horizons were also expanding. He became part of the circle around Reverend Stephen Matthew and his intellectual wife, Harriet. Blake was treated as an important man. He sang his poems to the appreciative company. The evenings at the Matthews didn't last long – Blake was too outspoken and self-opinionated to indulge in the art of conversation so celebrated by his contemporaries. But he immortalised the dissenters and cranks he met at the Matthews' in 1784 in a satirical poem, 'An Island in the Moon'.

Blake was still poor. John Flaxman had to pay for the first publication of his poetry, *Poetical Sketches*, in 1783. The collection, which included some poems written when Blake was a child, had a radical edge:

'When souls are torn to everlasting fire,
And fiends of Hell rejoice upon the slain,
O who can stand? Who hath caused this?
O who can answer at the throne of God?
The Kings and Nobles of the Land have done it!
Hear it not, Heave, thy Ministers have done it!'

A wealthy young man called John Hawkins tried to raise a subscription for Blake to go to Rome and study the great masters. Sadly Blake's subscription failed. He never had the chance that Flaxman and the painter Henry Fuseli did to see Italy's greatest art treasures. Henry Fuseli and Blake became close friends. Fuseli taught at the Royal Academy, where he was known for his sarcastic wit (he once advised a student to take his painting out to a field and shoot it). When Blake showed him one of his paintings, Fuseli commented, 'Now someone has told you this is very fine.' Blake replied, 'Yes. The Virgin Mary appeared to me, and told me it was very fine. What can you say to that?' Fuseli responded, 'Say? Why nothing – only her ladyship does not have immaculate taste'.[28] But Blake wrote of Fuseli:

'The only Man that e'er I knew
Who did not make me almost spew
Was Fuseli; he was both Turk & Jew
And so dear Christian Friends how do you do.'

In 1785 William and Catherine moved to lodgings in Poland Street, an area popular with artists, architects, bookbinders and sellers, musicians and poets. Some years later Percy Bysshe Shelley lived there. By 1788 Blake developed a new method of relief etching, which he believed was handed to him in a dream. It involved writing and drawing directly onto the copper plate, a process which was laborious because everything had to be done backwards. But it meant he could create flowing images and colour them brightly, a job Catherine helped with. The illuminated books he produced were influenced by medieval illuminated manuscripts. They are alive with the tendrils of vines, with birds, insects, fishes and beasts. His new technique was linked to his intention to produce grand, ornamental books at a price ordinary people could afford.[29]

The artistic and technical innovation went hand in hand with political and ideological tensions. Around this time Blake got to know Joseph Johnson, the foremost radical publisher of his day. Johnson's radical house guests included scientist Joseph Priestley, and the writers Tom Paine, Mary Wollstonecraft and William Godwin. Johnson thought Blake 'the most active, punctual and intelligent, as well as the most honest man in the trade'.[30] From 1779 to 1786 Johnson was Blake's best customer and one of his best friends.

Blake met some of Joseph Johnson's circle. He reputedly fell out with William Godwin after the philosopher borrowed money from him. Another writer suggests that Blake not only knew Mary Wollstonecraft but was in love with her.[31] Blake certainly had great admiration for Thomas

Paine. The government vilified Paine so badly that his friends jokingly called him 'demongorgon'.[32] But the more he was abused, the more Blake was drawn to his defence. One friend was certain that it was Blake who warned Paine to escape and take up his place in the revolutionary French assembly just before plans to arrest him could be carried out in 1792.[33]

Blake was, however, different from these radicals. Firstly, some thought him braver than them. After the French Revolution broke out in 1789, 'He courageously donned the famous symbol of liberty and equality – the bonnet rouge – in open day, and philosophically walked the streets with the same on his head. He is said to be the only one of the set who had the courage to make that profession of faith. Brave as a lion at heart was the meek spiritualist. Decorous Godwin, wily Paine, however much they might approve, paused before running the risk of a church-and-king mob at their heels'.[34]

Whatever the truth of this, Blake was certainly a deeply committed Christian whereas Johnson and his circle were deists, sceptics and atheists. They were rationalists who believed in scientific progress, while Blake thought reason limited the power of the imagination. They based their appeals on the power of reason, Blake based his on appeals to faith. Blake briefly joined the New Jerusalem Church, but he never joined or sympathised with any political organisation. But he was firmly embedded in the political network around Johnson's books. One biographer even suggests that 'he waged campaigns chiefly in the margins of the books he was reading' rather than trying to effect political change.[35]

Blake, however, shared many ideas with the radicals. The common ground was not in the field of political activity but in their understanding of aspects of society. Like Paine and Wollstonecraft, Blake understood that repression consists not only in political and military methods of forcing laws on populations. They shared a hatred of oppression's subtler tools – poor education, prejudice, habit, what Blake brilliantly called the 'mind-forged manacles'.[36]

Like the radicals, Blake was perplexed and enraged by the contradiction growing in the heart of his society. For the first time in history, new methods enabled the production of unlimited quantities of goods. Yet the majority of the population were poorer than ever and increasingly vulnerable to slumps which ruined them. The very people responsible for creating the potentially limitless wealth were forced into gruelling, repetitive work or into starvation for lack of work. There was a growing recognition that wealth for the few was based on the exploitation of the many. Blake understood how the whole establishment, monarchy, church, merchants and army all contributed to maintaining this system. He accused them all:

    'All the marks remain of the slave's scourge
    & tyrant's Crown,
    And of the Priest's o'ergorged Abdomen,
    & of the merchant's thin
    Sinewy deception, & of the warrior's outbraving
    & thoughtlessness
    In lineaments too extended & in bones too strait & long.
    They shew their wounds: they accuse.'

Writers as diverse as Mary Wollstonecraft and later Karl Marx analysed the experience of alienation, of the reduction of humanity to the level of machinery. Blake understood as a lived experience how the new capitalist methods of production sucked the energy and creativity out of the labourers. He saw how the new techniques separated artistic creativity from the manufacture of mass products. He expressed poetically what Marx would later express scientifically: 'Instead of developing the potential inherent in man's power, capitalist labour consumes these powers without replenishing them, burns them up as if they were a fuel, and leaves the individual workers the poorer'.[37] Blake would also have understood how the labourers create an alien world which comes to dominate them. His response, in the absence of seeing any earthly solution, was to retreat into his inner world.

The other radicals were more optimistic. They retained a faith in progress of reason and the perfectibility of humanity. Blake emphatically rejected the possibility of finding hope from this direction. Blake believed that reason was a brake on human imagination and energy: 'Reason is the bound or outward circumference of Energy' – and energy loathed the restraint. Blake felt that reason and science represented only a tiny part of reality and divine revelation was a far better guide to the universe, although A L Morton suggests this poem reveals Blake's dialectical approach to science:

'Mock on, Mock on Voltaire, Rousseau:
Mock on, Mock on: 'tis all in vain!
You throw the sand against the wind,
And the wind blows it back again.

And every sand becomes a Gem
Reflected in the beams divine;
Blown back they blind the mocking Eye,
But still in Israel's paths they shine
The Atoms of Democritus
And Newton's Particles of light
Are sands upon the Red sea shore,
Where Israel's tents do shine so bright.'

Blake was not simply reflecting the views of his dissenting contemporaries. The dissenting academies taught better science than the established universities. Blake rejected all this and isolated himself from his friends. His friend Henry Crabb Robinson once said Blake's 'religious convictions had brought on him the credit of being an absolute lunatic'.[38] In Blake's experience the products of rational inquiry had not freed men from superstition. On the contrary, they had created the means to enslave human beings further to the machinery of exploitation:

'O Satan my youngest born, art thou not Prince of
    the Starry Hosts
And of the Wheels of Heaven, to turn the Mills
    day & night?
Art thou not Newton Pantocrator weaving
    the Woof of Locke
To Mortals thy Mills seem everything.'

To Blake the Enlightenment, Newton and Locke, did not help people to understand and control their world. They

were the weapons used to reduce artisans like him to a state
of dependence.

Dark satanic mills
The companion of angels

Blake's adored younger brother Robert died of consumption
in spring 1787. He was aged 20. Blake's refusal to lose his
brother compelled him ever further towards the spirit world.
He used Robert's notebook (Robert was also an engraver),
drawing some of his most important designs on its pages. He
conversed with Robert daily for the rest of his life: 'even in
this world by it I am the companion of Angels'.

William and Catherine actively sought this exalted company. In April 1789 they were invited along with 70 or so others
to a meeting in the Swedenborg chapel in Great East Cheap.
They attended the five day long conference. The Blakes, like
many of their contemporaries, debated religious ideas. The
different sects had subversive aspects, in their rejection of
morality and authority. However, the tradition of the 17th
century was stamped with the defeat of the revolution and the
resulting retreat into mysticism. The Swedenborgians
believed in mystical experiences but the faithful were soon
arguing furiously about, predictably, sex and politics (in the
shape of the French Revolution). Some have found
Swedenborg 'boring and ridiculous'.[39] Eventually Blake
rejected Swedenborg because of his belief in predestination
but theological debates continued to shape his ideas.

Blake's interior world seemed as real to him as the physical world. He not only had visions of the dead, he conversed with them as regularly, if not more so, than he did with the living. He was not the only one. Catherine had visions and his sober, respectable brother James saw visions of Abraham and Moses.[40] Blake's imaginary guests were as welcome as his flesh and blood friends. John Milton, the poet of the 17th century English Revolution, was a regular visitor. Like Milton, who saw 'all God's men become prophets' during the English Revolution, Blake believed, 'Every honest man is a prophet; he utters his opinion both of private & public matters.'

One literary historian has suggested that Blake's visions may have been a tactic employed by a struggling artist to attract attention.[41] If so, it was not a very successful strategy. Genteel society called him mad. One admirer described Blake as 'quite mad, but of a madness that was really the elements of great genius ill-sorted: in fact a genius with a screw loose, as we used to say'.[42] With friends like that…

Blake was called a lunatic by those who could not understand his refusal to compromise his art for commercial success. He was labelled insane by once-radical gentlemen who could not comprehend why he never reneged on the revolutionary enthusiasms of his youth. Blake was occasionally depressed by the insults directed at him, but he did not really seek approval from his peers: he was writing for eternity. He understood that, 'There are States in which all Visionary Men are accounted Mad Men.'

Blake's poetic imagination was stimulated by his physical surroundings as well as his hallucinations. At the end of 1790

William and Catherine moved to Hercules Buildings in Lambeth. This was near Westminster Bridge but remained a rural area. Their house was very respectable and they could entertain their friends in some style. They also had a much loved garden, planted with figs and grapes. Blake saw Lambeth as 'the place of the Lamb' and a site for a new Jerusalem. When a rather prudish friend visited his house one day, he was shocked to find William and Catherine naked in their garden. Catherine was reading aloud from Milton's 'Paradise Lost'. Blake told his friend, 'It's only Adam and Eve, you know.' The Blakes found the divine in all aspects of human life, including their own bodies, and were happy to enjoy and celebrate it. Another incident shows how Blake could never stand by while the weak were suffering. One day Blake saw a boy shackled in a neighbour's garden and remonstrated passionately with his neighbour until the boy was freed.

Lambeth was no rural idyll. Near their house was a stone factory, a wine factory, potteries, a dye-works and lime kilns. Images of all these found their way into Blake's poems. The most famous building in the area, however, was the Albion Mill, built near Blackfriars Bridge and so near the Blakes' home. It was one of London's most popular tourist attractions. Erasmus Darwin described the mill as 'a grand and successful effort of human art'.[43] It was burnt down only a few years after it was built, to some rejoicing from its small local competitors. Peter Ackroyd imagines Blake walking past the burnt-out mill as he walked into the city, conjuring up his unforgetable images of dark satanic mills.

However free Blake was in his imagination, he remained dependent on others for his living. Occasionally the projects he engaged in could be artistically as well as financially rewarding. In 1791 Joseph Johnson secured him a commission to make his own designs for Mary Wollstonecraft's *Original Stories from Life* and to engrave Fuseli's illustrations for Erasmus Darwin's *The Botanic Garden*. He also began working on illustrations for the memoirs of a retired soldier, John Gabriel Stedman. Stedman called his work *Narrative of a Five Years Expedition, against the Revolted Negroes of Surinam*. Illustrating this book had a profound effect on William's attitude to the impact of the slave trade on black people and, by association, the enslavement of women and of humanity as a whole. Blake produced some of the most powerful images of the inhuman barbarity of slavery ever created. And closer to home another, greater revolt was claiming Blake's attention.

The tyrants fall

The fall of the Bastille in 1789 was the occasion for great rejoicing among English liberals and radicals. 'In fact, virtually every person of education, talent and enlightenment sympathised with the revolution, at all events until the Jacobin dictatorship, and often for very much longer'.[44] Throughout the 1790s the winds of freedom blew through the English chapels. Many among the congregations passed from dissent, to deism, to secularism and active politics. One preacher, William Huntingdon, complained about his congregation: 'Young and old, are breathing out slaughter against the ruling powers. Tom Paine and Satan have stuffed their heads full of politics'.[45]

Blake, like thousands of others, saw the dawn of a new world. A young William Wordsworth wrote, 'Bliss it was in that dawn to be alive, but to be young was very heaven.' Such revolutionary enthusiasm was everywhere, the hope of a different society was in everyone. The Marseillaise was sung in democratic clubs and societies, 'Liberty and Equality' was chalked on walls in London's streets. Inspired by events, Blake dashed off his 'Song of Liberty'. This work was no mystical fable but a description of the revolution and a call for the world to follow suit. The poem concluded, 'EMPIRE IS NO MORE! AND NOW THE LION AND THE LAMB SHALL CEASE!'

Blake's next poem, *The French Revolution*, was the only book he designed to be printed, ie mass produced, not etched. It was written in a more accessible style than any of Blake's books and was based on John Milton's great epic of revolution, 'Paradise Lost'. Joseph Johnson was to publish it and an existing proof copy of the first book exists dated 1791. But it was never published. Perhaps Johnson was afraid. He gave up printing Paine's *Rights of Man* in 1791. Johnson did go on to print books by Wollstonecraft and Godwin, because the government did not feel threatened by highly priced books like theirs. Ackroyd suggests that Blake may himself have withdrawn the book, from a 'neurotic' fear of prosecution or persecution. But such fears were not neurotic. Both Thomas Paine and Joseph Johnson were prosecuted in the following years. In fact, over 100 booksellers were prosecuted for selling Paine's work in a vendetta that lasted over 30 years.

In August 1972 the Parisian crowd, led by working women, stormed the Tuileries. The first executions of royalists in what became known as the 'Terror' began in September. In response to this, but with more than an eye on growing agitation at home, the prime minister announced the first new law against seditious writings. The reign of terror had begun in England. The execution of the French king in 1793 polarised English politics. While middle class liberals ran for cover, many working people continued to support the revolution. In 1795 some 200,000 protested against poverty, war, and the king.[46] With the suspension of habeas corpus, acts against meetings, combination and treasonable practices as well as the censorship of the press, radical writers had good reason to be afraid. Members of the working class reform group, the London Corresponding Society, were charged with treason.

By 1796 however, counter-revolution within France helped by hostile armies from outside defeated the revolution and Napoleon took over. There was widespread demoralisation among radicals. What Mary Wollstonecraft had feared when she visited Paris in 1793 had happened: 'If the aristocracy of birth is levelled with the ground, only to make room for that of riches, I am afraid that the morals of the people will not be much improved by the change, or the government rendered less venal'.[47]

The political nature of Blake's response to the French Revolution has been argued over by his biographers. After the withdrawal of *The French Revolution*, Blake gave up his hopes of reaching a mass audience and retreated into more obscure and private language. He may well have been intimidated. Hysteria was in the air. Town after town formed citizens' associations to suppress radical meetings and seditious writings. One was formed in the parish of Lambeth. Royalist mobs marched across London in October 1793 burning effigies of Tom Paine. One such mob marched very close to Hercules Buildings. These crowds beat up anyone who opposed them, and Blake had no wealth, status or servants to protect him.[48]

Ackroyd suggests that Blake had already given up on political activity and become a quietist, interested only in his own inner world. To support this view Ackroyd cites a letter in which Blake wrote, 'I am really sorry to see my Countrymen trouble themselves about Politics. If Men were wise the Most arbitrary Princes could not hurt them. If they are not Wise the Freest Government is compelled to be a Tyranny. Princes appear to me to be Fools Houses of Commons & Houses of Lords appear to me to be fools they seem to me to be something Else besides human life.' This letter was actually written to Samuel Palmer many years after the French Revolution. The politics he rejects are precisely the constitutional politics closed to men of his class and rendered redundant to radicals by the example of the revolution.

Ackroyd goes on to say that Blake 'believed only in the efficacy of individual virtue or enlightenment, and he displays not the slightest interest in any particular political or social philosophy'.[49] This is a misunderstanding of Blake, and the relationship between his religious beliefs and his political hopes. The work Blake produced in the years following the French Revolution is brimming with political, social and philosophical views. The arguments that raged following the revolution found their way into Blake's poems directly. In 1793, for example, Blake wrote in his *Poems from the Notebook* (or Rossetti Manuscript) about a serpent that forced its way into a chapel of gold:

'Vomiting his poison out
On the bread & on the wine.
So I turn'd into a sty
And laid me down among the swine.'

A ferocious debate was then raging about the 'swinish multitude', an insult Edmund Burke hurled at the French masses. Blake cannot have been unaware of the implications of these words. He answered the corruption of the church by siding with the swine.

In addition to the direct references to political debates, the development of the revolution inspired and stimulated all the amazing outpouring of work he produced in the decade after the fall of the Bastille.

The price of experience

The impact of the revolution and England's war against France was to propel Blake from innocence to experience. He understood that 'experience' was born from struggle and the defeat of the poor. In 'Vala' he wrote:
'What is the price of Experience? do men buy it
for a song?
Or wisdom for a dance in the street? No, it is bought
with the price
Of all that a man hath, his house, his wife, his children.
Wisdom is sold in the desolate market where none
come to buy,

And in the wither'd field where the farmer plows for bread in vain.'

Blake published his major works in the years that followed the revolution. First came 'Tiriel', an illustrated poem which tells the story of an old blind king who rejects his children, part George III, part King Lear. The poem draws on contemporary debates about education developed by Jean-Jacques Rousseau and Mary Wollstonecraft. Then came 'The Book of Thel', which tells of how Thel the shepherdess uses her reason to probe the meaning of life. Because she is just rational, she is defeated and flees from a terrifying vision of her own mortality (although the illustrations show a more positive ending). Blake's brilliant *Songs of Innocence*, discussed below with its companion volume, *Songs of Experience*, was also published in 1789.

The following year Blake published *The Marriage of Heaven and Hell*, a spectacular example of how the French Revolution inspired Blake. 'This book is an expression of Blake's mood of sympathy with the revolution, seen as the expression of the irrepressible energy of life'.[50] David Erdman writes that *The Marriage* describes the French Revolution, from its first phase of joyous optimism, the 'Roses planted where thorns did grow', to the bloody counter-revolution, 'the sneaking serpent'.[51] It is also the product of Blake's spiritual turmoil. He decided that the Swedenborgians were superficial because they only conversed with religious angels and not with devils.[52] The poem also drew on the 'controversialists', like Constantin Volney in

The Ruins, or a Survey of the Revolutions of Empire and Tom Paine's *Age of Reason*. These freethinkers' books attacked the Old Testament. The poem centres on a debate between angels and devils in which the devils get all the best lines. *The Marriage* is constructed around a series of brilliant epigrams that celebrate energy, experience, and sexuality:

'Exuberance is Beauty.'

'The road to excess leads to the palace of wisdom.'

'Without contraries, there is no progress.'

'The nakedness of woman is the work of God.'

'Energy is eternal delight.'

'Everything that lives is holy.'

'Better to kill an infant in its cradle than nurse unacted desires.'

'Prisons are built with stones of Law, Brothels with bricks of Religion.'

'The tygers of wrath are wiser than the horses of instruction.'

The Marriage was written 20 years before the German philosopher George Hegel developed his idea of the dialectic. In this vision we have the same sense of a society torn by contradictions and at war with itself that Hegel then Karl Marx drew on decades later.

'A Song of Liberty' at the end of *The Marriage* celebrates the casting out of French monarchy and the victory of the revolutionary forces at the battle of Valmy. As the republic was being announced in Paris, Blake was writing the climactic lines, 'Empire is no more!'

The *Songs of Innocence* are some of Blake's most popular poems. The book's illustrations are bursting with life, with figures leaping, running and flying as if released from their physical constraints. The songs are sung by innocents, joyful babies, children, pretty robins and animals who all find protection, nurturing and love. If the poems are put in their social context, new and more sinister meanings appear. During Blake's lifetime there was a growing awareness of the piteous condition of thousands of English children. Children were no longer apprenticed as Blake had been: they were sent to the factories in their thousands. In 1802 an Act of Parliament limited the working day to 12 hours for children raised by the parish. It took until 1819 until free children were granted the same protection. With the knowledge of all those stolen childhoods in mind, read the end of 'The School Boy', which tells of 'little ones that spend the day, in sighing and dismay' just like those factory children:

'…How can the bird that is born for joy
Sit in a cage and sing?
How can a child, when fears annoy,
But droop his tender wing,
And forget his youthful spring?

O! father & mother, if buds are nip'd
And blossoms blown away,
And if the tender plants are strip'd
Of their joy in the springtime day,
By sorrow and care's dismay,

How shall the summer arise in joy,

Or the summer fruits appear?
Or how shall we gather what griefs destroy,
Or bless the mellowing year,
When will the blasts of winter appear?'

James Blake sold clothes to the parish orphanage next to the Blake family home. The death rate for the children abandoned there was between 50 and 100 percent every year. With that atrocious barbarity in mind, read 'The Little Boy Lost':

'Father! Father! where are you going?
Oh, do not walk so fast.
Speak, father, speak to your little boy,
Or else I shall be lost.

The night was dark, no father was there;
The child was wet with dew;
The mire was deep, & the child did weep,
And away the vapour flew.'

The plight of chimney sweeps scandalised even brutal 18th century London. Boys were bought as young as four. They were burnt, suffocated and beaten into sweeping chimneys, and their reward was deformity, cancer, destitution and death. They were a symbol of sexual availability, thus the custom of sweeps kissing brides.[53] During May Day celebrations sweeps were allowed one day of freedom and pleasure. Blake's poem 'The Chimney Sweeper' describes the misery and false comfort offered to the boys:

'When my mother died I was very young,
And my Father sold me while yet my tongue

Could scarcely cry "weep! weep! weep! weep!"
So your chimneys I sweep & in soot I sleep…'

The sweep dreams his friends are dead and in coffins:
'And by came an Angel who had a bright key,
And he open'd the coffins and set them all free;
Then down a green plain leaping, laughing, they run,
And wash in a river, and shine in the Sun.

Then naked & white, all their bags left behind,
They rise upon clouds and sport in the wind;
And the Angel told Tom, if he'd be a good boy,
He'd have God for his father and never want joy.

And so Tom awoke; and we rose in the dark,
And got with our bags & and our brushes to work.
Tho' the morning was cold, Tom was happy & warm;
So if all do their duty they need not fear harm.'

If the *Songs of Innocence* have shades of menace, the *Songs of Experience* are downright dark and disturbing. 'The Chimney Sweeper' in *Experience* lays savagely bare what is ironically suggested in *Innocence*. The last verse is:
'And because I am happy & dance & sing,
They think they have done me no injury,
And are gone to praise God & his Priest & King,
Who make up a heaven of our misery.'

The children of *Innocence* who are found reappear in *Experience*, enslaved, sick and full of sorrow. The *Songs of Experience*, written in Robert's old notebook during 1793, are a lament for the abandoned, friendless and betrayed. The poems are built around a series of oppositions and contrasts such as innocence and experience, love and hate, energy and passivity, freedom and restraint. Contrast, for example, these two poems. The first, 'The Divine Image', is an account of Blake's religious philosophy that all that is holy exists in all people, whatever their race:

'To Mercy, Pity, Peace and Love
All pray in their distress;
And to these virtues of delight
Return their thankfulness.

For Mercy, Pity, Peace and Love
Is God, our father dear,
And Mercy, Pity, Peace and Love
Is Man, his care and child.

For Mercy has a human heart,
Pity a human face,
And Love, the human form divine,
And Peace the human dress.

Then every man, of every clime,
That prays in this distress,
Prays to the human form divine,
Love, Mercy, Pity, Peace,

And all must love the human form,
In heathen, turk, or jew;
Where Mercy, Love, & Pity dwell
There God is dwelling too.'

An additional poem in *Songs of Experience* (etched about 1794), 'A Divine Image', shows movement from innocence to corruption, from goodness to evil:

'Cruelty has a Human Heart,
And Jealousy a Human Face;
Terror the Human Form Divine,
And Secrecy the Human Dress.

The Human Dress is forged Iron,
The Human Form a fiery Forge,
The Human Face a Furnace seal'd,
The Human Heart its hungry Gorge.'

The two books mark a dramatic shift, from lyrical ambiguity to categorical condemnation of society. From *Experience*, the poem 'London' is a marvellous condemnation of inequality and the impact of the market. It is passionate, simple and clear – and it could only have been written by someone who lived among the victims of London society:

'I wander thro' each chartered street
Near where the chartered Thames does flow
And mark in every face I meet
Marks of weakness, marks of woe.

In every cry of every man,
In every infant's cry of fear
In every voice, in every ban,
The mind-forged manacles I hear.

How the chimney sweeper's cry
Every black'ning Church appalls;

And the hapless soldier's sigh
Runs in blood down palace walls

But most thro' midnight streets I hear
How the youthful harlot's curse
Blasts the new-born infant's tear
And blights with plagues the marriage hearse.'

This poem links society's key institutions, the church, marriage and the army, with their victims, the chimney sweep, the prostitute and the soldier. It builds on Blake's brilliant metaphor of mind-forged manacles, the ideas that encourage people to accept their lot in life. Its language relates directly to contemporary debates about the French Revolution. E P Thompson explained that 'chartered' was a 'generalised symbolic power'. It refers to the filthy business of commerce, to chartered companies like the Dutch East India Company. It also refers to fiercely debated charters of constitutional rights and liberties. Opponents of the revolution, like Edmund Burke, wanted exclusive and limited rights for privileged citizens. Radicals like Tom Paine wanted universal human rights.[54]

The shift from innocence to experience was not just a personal journey for Blake. It was a journey undertaken by the French women who wanted bread and found they had to conquer an army to get it, by revolutionaries who wanted justice and ended up killing a king to get it, by English liberals who celebrated French liberty and fraternity but learnt that they could not be won without the use of force. Some of these impulses can be seen in one of Blake's most popular poems, 'Tyger':

'Tyger, tyger! burning bright
In the forests of the night,
What immortal hand or eye
Could frame thy fearful symmetry?

In what distant deeps or skies
Burnt the fire of thine eyes?
On what wings dare he aspire?
What the hand dare seize the fire?

And what shoulder, & what art,
Could twist the sinews of thy heart?
And when thy heart began to beat,
What dread hand? & what dread feet?

What the hammer? what the chain?
In what furnace was thy brain?
What the anvil? what dread grasp
Dare its deadly terrors clasp?

When the stars threw down their spears,
And water'd heaven with their tears,
Did he smile his work to see?
Did he who made the Lamb make thee?

Tyger! Tyger! burning bright
In the forests of the night,
What immortal hand or eye
Dare frame thy fearful symmetry?'

Blake uses the imagery of the Bible, of Rousseau's noble savage, but above all of the French Revolution. While he was writing the poem the revolutionaries were being abused as wild beasts and their leaders were compared to savage tigers. There are also industrial images. The hammer, anvil and furnaces speak of exploited human creativity as well as divine creation.

Blake's next major poem, published in 1793, was 'The Vision of the Daughters of Albion'. It express Blake's hopes for sexual liberation directly and his hopes for political liberation indirectly through images of the sexual fulfilment of female nations. In the poem Oothoon is raped by Bromion, a brutal slave owner. Violated, she is rejected by her beloved Theotormon. Oothoon is a victim of the attitudes to women Mary Wollstonecraft challenged the previous year in her *A Vindication of the Rights of Woman*. Oothoon cannot free herself, but her arguments against religion and against oppression were political statements. Some of these ideas were developed in 'America: A Prophecy', also published in 1793. 'America' tells the story of the anti-colonial revolt. It introduces Orc, the embodiment of energy and rebellion, who faces up to Urizen, the tyrant and priest. These characters became pillars of Blake's prophetic poems. 'America' ends with a final transformation which brings liberation to the most oppressed, the black slaves:

'Let the slave grinding at the mill, run out into the field;
Let him look up into the heavens & laugh in the
    bright air;
Let the inchained soul, shut up in darkness and in
    sighing,

Whose face has never seen a smile in thirty weary years,
Rise and look out; his chains are loose, his dungeon
   doors are open;
And let his wife and children return from the
   oppressor's scourge.'

In 1794, Blake published *Europe*, an extraordinarily beautiful illustrated book. It tells the story of oppression and revolution, the horrors of war and repression. It evokes the sense
of persecution endured by radicals like Blake as the British
government set up a system of spies:

   'Every house a den, every man bound: the shadows
      are fill'd
   With spectres, and the windows wove over with
      curses of iron:
   Over the doors "Thou shalt not", & over the chimneys
   "Fear"
      is written:
   With bands of iron round their necks fasten'd
      into the walls
   The citizens, in leaden gyves the inhabitants of suburbs
   Walk heavy; soft and bent are the bones of the villages.'

Other prophetic books followed, including the bloodthirsty
Urizen. Urizen the tyrant provokes a rebellion in heaven and
a complex family battle among the gods. The text has been
interpreted as an attack on the Old Testament incorporating
the contemporary language of revolution.[55] All Blake's
prophetic books showed an unjust, cruel and oppressive

world in which dreams of freedom are never realised. This vision of the world was shaped by a revolution that promised liberty and equality and ended up defeated and devouring its own makers. Blake began to retreat into the complex, at times impenetrable, highly personal world of his prophetic books. One of his favourite symbols was Albion, the ancient name for England. Albion represents an innocent primitive Eden, now fallen into decay under the control of reactionary forces, symbolised by Los and Enitharmon. Los and Enitharmon become the masters of looms and furnaces. Orc is an activist, symbol of revolutionary energy. Urizen is the creator, the lonely lawgiver, and unforgiving prophet.

Even Blake's mythical characters reveal something of the brutal life of the labouring poor and the horrors of the 19th century factory:

'cruel works of many Wheels I view,
wheel without wheel, with cogs tyrannic
Moving by compulsion each other, not as those
in Eden, which,
Wheel within wheel in freedom revolve in harmony
& peace.'

In his weird and mystical way Blake expressed the impact of machines that had the potential to liberate people from drudgery but instead threw workers back into barbarism. Marx made the same point: 'Machinery, gifted with the wonderful power of shortening and fructifying human labour, we behold starving and overworking it. The newfangled sources of wealth, by some strange weird spell, are turned into sources of want. The victories of art seem bought by loss of character'.[56]

But Blake did not only write increasingly obscure prophecies. As the English government began to concentrate on its domestic conflict against the poor, so Blake began to describe it. During 1795 he wrote 'The Song of Los', a simple, direct poem very unlike the prophetic books. In 'Los' Blake wrote about famine that was man-made, about the urban poor who starved while the rich prospered, and of the Royalist mobs incited to intimidate radicals. The house of dissenting scientist Joseph Priestley was burnt down by such a mob in Birmingham in 1791. While Thomas Hardy of the London Correspondence Society was in prison on treason charges his heavily pregnant wife was killed when she jumped from a window to escape a similar crowd in 1794.[57]

'Shall not the King call for Famine from the heath,
Nor the Priest for Pestilence from the fen,
To restrain, to dismay, to thin
The inhabitant of mountain and plain,
In the day, of full-feeding prosperity
And the night of delicious songs?
Shall not the Councellor throw his curb
Of Poverty on the laborious,
To fix the price of labour,
To invent allegoric riches?
And the privy admonishers of men
Call for fires in the City,
For heaps of smoking ruins
In the night of prosperity & wantonness?

To turn man from his path,
To restrain the child from the womb,
To cut off the bread from the city,
That the remnant may learn to obey,
That the pride of the heart may fail,
That the lust of the eyes may be quench'd,
That the delicate ear in its infancy
May be dull'd, and the nostrils clos'd up,
To teach mortal worms the path
That leads from the gates of the Grave?'

Blake knew something of the hard path to the gates of the grave. He created some great work in the 1790s, but he never stopped depending on commercial commissions for his livelihood. He undertook to engrave designs for Edward Young's *Night Thoughts* in 1795. Blake threw himself into the project body and soul, encouraged by a visit from archangel Gabriel. It was an ambitious and extravagant book – but it sank like a stone, unreviewed, unremarked, unnoticed. The war with France meant little spare cash for luxuries like art. The failure was a financial disaster for Blake, a personal blow dealt him by the counter-revolutionary war.

THE RULE OF THE BEAST

IN JUNE 1793 BLAKE wrote, 'I say I shan't live five years, And if I live it will be a wonder.' He was still alive five years later, but with no more confidence in his future. He wrote, 'To defend the Bible in this year of 1798 would cost a man his life.' One episode from those years shows why Blake was right to be nervous. The government were worried that they were losing the propaganda war to the radicals. They prompted one Richard Watson to write a response to Thomas Paine. Watson had been a radical known as the 'levelling prelate'. He settled his differences with authority, became the Bishop of Llandaff and wrote a pamphlet recanting his past beliefs and denouncing the French Revolution.

Nothing annoys radicals like a turncoat and Watson's attack on Paine caused outrage on the left. William Wordsworth wrote a reply to the bishop blaming his camp for violence: 'Left to the quiet exercise of their own judgement, do you think that the people would have thought it necessary to set fire to the house of the philosophic

Priestley?' If Wordsworth was angry, Blake was absolutely fuming. He wrote, 'I have not the Charity for the Bishop that he pretends to have for Paine. I believe him to be a State trickster. Dishonest misrepresentation. Priestly Impudence. Comtemptible Falsehood & Detraction. Presumptuous Monster. The Beast and the Whore rule without control.' He added, 'It appears to me now that Tom Paine is a better Christian than the Bishop.'

Neither Wordsworth or Blake were brave enough to publish their relies to the bishop. Another radical did publish an attack on Watson. Because of his article, Gilbert Wakefield was thrown into prison from 1799 to 1801 and died soon after his release, broken by the vicious imprisonment. Joseph Johnson was prosecuted in 1798 – for selling Wakefield's work. This story shows that Blake was not paranoid, but a man who understood what his enemies were capable of.

The bishop was not the only eminent public figure to elicit a response from Blake. Thomas Malthus argued in his 1798 *An Essay on the Principle of Population* that overpopulation caused poverty. Blake responded angrily:

'When a man looks pale
With labour & abstinence, say he looks healthy and
happy;
And when his children sicken, let them die; there are
enough
Born, even too many, & our Earth will be overrun
Without these arts.
Preach temperance: say he is overgorg'd &

drowns his wit
In strong drink, tho' you know that bread & water are all
He can afford.'

That year of 1798 saw real as well as ideological conflicts. It was the year of brutal repression in Ireland, the first executions of radicals for treason in England and France's invasion of neutral Switzerland. One royalist wrote with great satisfaction how all this was 'great enough to bring any Jacobin to his senses'. The political atmosphere and the hardship of the war years had drained dry the limited market that existed for Blake's work. This fiercely independent man became totally dependent on his friends. John Flaxman helped by commissioning Blake to make pretty, playful illustrations of Thomas Gray's poems for his wife Nancy. In 1799 Blake met his great patron and family friend Thomas Butts and his wife Elizabeth. Butts bought all his poetry, arranged commissions for him and promoted his work. William Hayley, a gentleman-poet, was another important friend to Blake. Robert Southey wrote about Hayley, 'Everything about that man was good except his poetry'.[58] Hayley was happy to care for the brilliant, despised, honest artisan William Blake.

His support was very timely. The year 1800 was a desperate year for the supporters of the revolution. Some radicals were dead, including Mary Wollstonecraft, some had fled, Joseph Priestley to America and Thomas Paine to France. Only a few like Joseph Johnson stayed put. The government was afraid of writers and but increasingly they were afraid of the masses and even of the militia (they dared not station barracks near manufacturing towns in case the people infected the soldiers with unrest). Blake was deeply depressed. The combination of political and professional disappointment was a lot for him to bear.

Flaxman helped to arrange for William and Catherine to move to a rented cottage close to Hayley, in Felpham on the Sussex coast. Blake was conscious of his vulnerability. He wrote to Flaxman, full of thanks for his escape:

> 'The American War began. All its dark horrors passed before my face
> Across the Atlantic to France. Then the French Revolution commenc'd in thick clouds,
> And My Angels have told me that seeing such visions I could not subsist on the Earth,
> But by my conjunction with Flaxman, who knows to forgive
> Nervous Fear.'

Blake hoped for relief from his nervous fears. He wanted to escape from the brutality of London physically as he had retreated from human society in his work. He wanted the beauty and freedom of the countryside and the seashore:

> 'Rending the manacles of Londons Dungeon dark
> I have rent the black net & escap'd. See My Cottage at Felpham in joy
> Beams over the sea a bright light over France, but the Web & the Veil I have left
> Behind me at London resists every beam of light; hanging from heaven to Earth

Dropping with human gore. Lo! I have left it! I have
    torn it from my limbs.
I shake my wings ready to take my flight!'

A wicked and seditious man

But even this idyll was not safe from political conflicts. By
August 1803 fears of a French invasion were running so high
that women were ordered away from the south coast. The
peace of Felpham was shattered by the arrival of 75 soldiers,
to be billeted among the 80 villages. Blake was not the only
local to find their presence offensive and distressing. Locals
refused to volunteer and rebellion was stirred by handbills,
circulated around the village.

   One morning Blake found a couple of soldiers lounging
around in his garden. Blake forcibly marched them out and a
few months later found himself on trial for sedition. One soldier accused Blake of being a military painter, having misheard the description miniature painter. Bad hearing seems
to be a common complaint among government employees.
Another spy sent to eavesdrop on Wordsworth and
Coleridge was nicknamed Spy Nozy, after he misheard their
conversation about the philosopher Spinoza.

   The charges made by the soldiers were very serious. They
included inviting 'the Enemies of our said Lord the King to
invade this Realm and Unlawfully and Wickedly to seduce
and encourage his Majesty's Subjects to resist and oppose our
said Lord the King'.[59] The sentence could be imprisonment

or even execution. Catherine was not included in the formal charges, but she was mentioned in the soldier's testimony. He reported that, 'Blake said, My Dear, you would not fight against France – she replied no, I would for Bonaparte as long as I am able.' Blake's bail was set at £250, a huge amount that reflected the severity of the charge.

On 4 October the first trial took place at Petworth. Blake was horrified when the jury found him to be a wicked, seditious and evil person and ruled that Blake had badly beaten the soldier even though this was not part of the charges against Blake! The case was sent to trial in January 1804, at the Chichester sessions. Blake had moved back to London and had to travel to Chichester, fearing rumours about his radicalism would reach the town. Catherine was so traumatised Blake believed her at the 'Gates of Death'. The trial judge was Charles Lennox, third duke of Richmond and commander of the local militia. Lennox was satirised alongside Pitt as 'two reformers whose zeal had carried them into office but had not followed them there'.[60] The prosecutor emphasised 'the atrocity and malignity of the charge'.[61] To cap it all, Blake's defending barrister fell ill during trial.

It turned out that Blake was his own best advocate. He electrified the court by shouting 'false' at prosecuting witnesses. His witnesses were respectable and reputable, whereas the soldiers were dodgy drunks who contradicted each other. Blake was found not guilty and the court erupted into noisy exultations.[62] Blake exacted an eternal revenge on the soldier who accused him, Scofield, by roasting him in a furnace in everlasting damnation in his poems. Blake had escaped imprisonment, but he couldn't escape ridicule, disappointment and obscurity. When they moved back to London, the Blakes were poorer and more isolated than ever.

The prophet of Poverty Lane

William and Catherine found two small rooms to rent off Oxford Street, near Tyburn, backing onto grim Poverty Lane. They were to live here for the next 17 years. Despite their poor circumstances Blake could still enjoy moments of pure joy. In the autumn of 1804, when he visited the Truchsession Art Gallery, 'Oh glory, oh delight', he wrote to Hayley, 'excuse my enthusiasm or rather madness, for I am really drunk with intellectual vision whenever I take a pencil or graver to my hand, even as I used to be in my youth, and as I have not been for twenty dark, but very profitable years. I thank God that I courageously pursued my course through darkness.'

Blake was still seeking public acknowledgement of his artistic achievements. In 1809 he organised an exhibition in his brother James's shop. He produced a descriptive catalogue, but unfortunately forgot to put directions to the shop on it. Hardly anyone came. One reviewer who did see it wrote that Blake was an 'unfortunate lunatic' on the strength of what he saw. For all his otherwordliness, Blake was deeply hurt. He hit out at all his friends, patrons, booksellers and critics alike.

Even Blake's friends found it hard to help him. He had become so erratic and undependable and seemed incapable of meeting deadlines. Some attempts to help Blake made things worse. Hayley proposed publishing his own ballads with Blake's engravings. In the end Blake had to pay publication costs and many copies of the book were destroyed in a fire. Then, Robert Hartley Cromek, a young Yorkshire engraver, approached Blake about a new project. Some saw right through him. Novelist Walter Scott had him sussed: 'Cromek is a perfect Brain-sucker living upon the labours of others'.[63] Blake did some designs for Robert Blair's poem 'The Grave'. He was really excited, confident that the projected work would 'set me above the difficulties I have hitherto encountered'.

But just as Blake was anticipating a cash boost, Cromek was complaining that Blake's work was 'too much of the mind and too little of the hand' to be generally understood.[64] Blake's designs were used, but they were actually engraved by another man, Luigi Schiavonetti. 'The Grave' earned Blake only £21 and some more abusive reviews in magazines like *The Examiner*. Blake took his revenge in the only way he could, with his pen:

'Poor Schiavonetti died of the Cromek
A thing thats tied about the Examiner's neck
Who cries all art is fraud & Genius a trick
And Blake is an unfortunate Lunatic.'

Amazingly, Blake forged a poetical rebirth out of the bitterness of betrayal and ridicule. He reworked 'Vala', begun in 1796, into 'The Four Zoas', finished around 1807. This is a dense and complex work, but its imagery depends on Blake's endless disgust at the society around him. Blake contrasts the

labours of shepherds in rural, pre-industrial society who
work in harmony with their wheels and ploughs with the
with the enslavement of labourers to the machinery of capitalist manufacturing:

> 'And in their stead, intricate wheels invented, wheel
>   without wheel,
> To perplex youth in their outgoings & to bind to
>   labours in Albion
> Of day & night the myriads of eternity: that they may
>   grind
> And polish brass & iron hour after hour, laborious task,
> Kept ignorant of its use: that they might spend the
>   days of wisdom
> In sorrowful drudgery to obtain a scanty pittance
>   of bread,
> In ignorance to view a small portion & think that All
> And call it Demonstration, blind to all the simple rules of
>   life.'

There were only a few factories in England when Blake was
writing, but somehow he understood how the methods
created by human beings would come to utterly dominate
them. Physically, labourers would be bound to the rhythm
of machines. Mentally, they would become alienated from
the creative powers they had realised through labour.
Their understanding of the world would be limited to their
own narrow experience at the expense of more general
awareness of society. Karl Marx later described this in his
theory of alienation.

This poem also shows Blake's condemnation of Britain's war was undimmed. He still predicted a revolutionary transformation for Britain. This illuminated manuscript was revised many times, each time apparently in response to developments in the war. This makes it a complex book, but one which contains some of Blake's most beautiful poetic visions of a society racked by exploitation and repression:

> 'The villages lament: they faint, outstretch'd upon the
>   plain.
> Wailing runs round the Valleys from the Mill & from the
>   Barn.
> But the most polish'd palaces, dark, silent, bow with
>   dread,
> Hiding their books & pictures underneath the dens of
>   the Earth.
> The Cities send to one another saying: "My sons are mad"
> With wine of cruelty. Let us plat a scourge, O Sister City.
> Children are nourish'd for the Slaughter; once the Child
>   was fed
> With Milk, but wherefore now are children fed with
>   blood?'

In 'Vala' Blake outlined his vision of a revolutionary uprising, where Los cries:

> 'Awake, O Brother Mountain!
> Let us refuse the Plow and Spade, the heavy Roller and
>   spiked
> Harrow; burn all these corn fields, throw down all these
>   fences!'

Society is corrupted by men who have lost their imagination and live in the thrall of material greed and the selfishness of those who promote the interests of their own families at the expense of the rest of the world. There is a cosmic antagonism between those who live in the 'tents of prosperity' and the 'captive in chains, & and the poor in the prison' and the rebellion of poor is always just. This illustrated book encapsulates the heart of Blake's uncompromising revolutionary outlook, tempered by the bitter experience of defeat and repression.

Although Blake was sensitive to industrial changes, politically his hopes had been crushed by the failure of the French Revolution. His trial further scared him away from politics. Blake is praised by his biographers for never reneging on his earlier radicalism. However, this steadfastness is not so impressive if Blake simply retreated into his private world, neither apostate nor activist, just isolated from all political debate. Paul Foot has pointed out that Blake held aloof from all the great issues of his later years.[65] To understand Blake's response to the pressure of those years, it helps to see him alongside his fellow poets, Robert Southey, Samuel Taylor Coleridge, who thought Blake a man of genius and a kindred spirit, and William Wordsworth, who copied Blake's poems out of a friend's book.

These educated gentlemen were a class above William Blake socially. Yet, like him, they were youthful revolutionary enthusiasts. Robert Southey had been expelled from school for editing an anti-flogging school magazine, *The Flagellant*. As students he and Samuel Taylor Coleridge had hatched a scheme to live together in a Pantisocracy, a secluded society without private property and governed equally by men and women. He supported the French Revolution, being a 'down-right, upright Republican', as Coleridge called him. Southey's play, *Wat Tyler*, was based on the Peasant Revolt of 1381, and his poem 'Thalaba the Destroyer' told of a revolution against a corrupt court. William Wordsworth did more than celebrate the French Revolution in verse. He travelled to revolutionary France, fell in love with a French woman, Annette Vallois, and had a child with her. His greatest friend and poetical collaborator was Samuel Taylor Coleridge, a drug addict and lay preacher. As a sixteen year old, Coleridge wrote his first poem, 'The Fall of the Bastille', which pointed to how the revolution could deepen with liberty's 'universal cry reaching the labourers of the field'.[66] In Bristol, Coleridge took up public speaking and achieved notoriety as a democrat and Jacobin sympathiser. His anti-war, anti slave trade rhetoric combined aspirations to a bloodless revolution with a Christian millenarianism very much like Blake's.

The progress of the counter-revolution in France left the poets caught in a contradiction. Their impulse towards radicalism, Jacobin sympathies, aspirations to liberty and the rule of reason competed with the reality of the French terror, the guillotine and Napoleon's dictatorship. They were champions of the French Revolution and yet were sickened by it; they championed the cause of the common people, yet they had reason to fear the mob.

Southey was the first of the poets to openly recant on his former radicalism, publicly ridiculing his former friends.

In 1812 poets such as Lord Byron condemned the brutal suppression of the Luddite rebels and frame breakers.[67] Southey had no such humanitarian qualms. He praised the army which 'preserves us from the most dreadful of all calamities, an insurrection of the poor against the rich'.[68] In 1813 he accepted the poet laureateship, but his past came back to haunt him. *Wat Tyler* was published in 1817 despite his desperate attempts to suppress it. It became his most popular work. Coleridge experienced doubts about his erstwhile radicalism in 1796, after the terror, when he wrote, 'I have snapped my squeaking baby trumpet of sedition and the fragments lie scattered'. Like Blake, Coleridge experienced a tendency to retreat into his self and into religion. Wordsworth's first real crisis of sympathy with the French Revolution came not with the terror, but with the rise of Napoleon. Once he was in power, France's war was no longer a war of self-defence, but a war of aggression. Once France was seen as aggressive, the British could be justified in going to war against France. From there it was a short step to patriotism and a wholesale accommodation with Britain's rulers.

For Coleridge and Wordsworth the French Revolution, the attempt to realise ideals, had ended in the opposite of everything they had hoped for. Both spent years trying to reconcile defeat in France and their desire to continue hoping change was possible. They tried to resist apostasy. In 1799 Coleridge complained to Wordsworth about those who 'in consequence of the complete failure of the French Revolution...have thrown up all hopes of the amelioration of mankind and are sinking under an almost epicurean self-ishness, disguising the same under the soft titles of domestic attachment and contempt for visionary philosophies'.[69]

A few years later Wordsworth expressed the same feeling in poetry:

'If in these times of fear,
This melancholy waste of hope o'erthrown,
If, 'mid indifference and apathy
And wicked exultation, when good men,
On every side fall off we know not how,
To selfishness, disguis'd in gentle names
Of peace, and quiet, and domestic love,
Yet mingled, not unwillingly, with sneers
On visionary minds; if in this time
Of dereliction and dismay, I yet
Despair not our nature; but retain
A more than Roman confidence, a faith
The fails not, in all sorrow my support.'

Ultimately Wordsworth and Coleridge lost their hopes and turned to domestic life and contempt for visionaries. Blake found no route back into a polite society which did not want his skills and disliked his art. And as A L Morton suggests, Blake never stopped seeking a revolutionary solution. What Blake had in common with Wordsworth and Coleridge and with the poet John Milton was an urgent necessity. At key turning points in their lives, they had to find new ways to express in art the turmoil of political defeat. Milton had writ-ten only revolutionary pamphlets for 20 years. After the restoration of the monarchy in 1688 he poured his experience of defeat and continued hope into the epic poems 'Paradise Lost' and 'Samson Agonistes'. Out of the French Revolution Wordsworth and Coleridge found a new poetic language and celebrated ordinary life in their *Lyrical Ballads*. Wordsworth explicitly linked his new style of poetry with the revolution not in art, but in society. Blake found the extraordinary, vivid images of his *Songs* and his engravings in the debris of his political hopes, not in isolation from society, but through engagement with it.

A ceaseless mental fight

In spring 1820, William and Catherine moved to nicer lodgings in Fountain Court, south of the Strand. Around this time, Blake was discovered by a group of young artists who called themselves The Ancients. The group included the artist Samuel Palmer, John Linnell, a well-off dissenter and enthusiast of great integrity, and John Varley, who encouraged Blake to draw his visionary heads. The Ancients called Blake the interpreter, their key to unlocking the mysteries of the old masters. Linnell helped Blake by organising work for him. When they found that Blake was having to sell precious prints, Linnell raised money from members of the Royal Academy and rich collectors.

Blake moved in some surprising circles during these years. Early in 1818 Blake was seen at a dinner party given by Lady Caroline Lamb, Byron's lover and London socialite. The society diarist Lady Charlotte Bury met Blake and admired him. She described him as 'full of beautiful imaginations and genius' and 'not a regular professional painter, but one of those persons who follow the art for its own sweet sake, and derive their happiness from its pursuit'.[70]

Such exalted company did not mean that Blake had made his peace with high society. During the years 1812-14 there were riots and hunger across England. An attempt was made to assassinate the Prince Regent. The resulting hysteria led to another raft of laws and the suspension of habeas corpus. Blake, however, continued his protest against the beast. In 1820 George III died and radicals rejoiced. Byron wrote with typically devastating wit:

'I grant his household abstinence, I grant
His neutral virtues, which most monarchs want;
I know he was a constant consort; own He was a
decent sire and middling lord,
All this is much, and most upon a throne.
I grant him all the kindest can accord:
And this was well for him, but not for those
Millions who found him what oppression chose.'

The coronation of the Prince Regent was marked by scandals about his lovers. Publicising his affairs was one way subversives found to ridicule the prince and the monarchy, just as it is today. Radical print-seller Isaac Barrow commissioned Blake to engrave a portrait of one of the prince's mistresses, Harriet Quentin. 'Blake was thus on the fringe of a sensational event and acting as the agent of a notoriously radical print-seller'.[71]

However, despite his slingshots against the establishment, the overwhelming theme of Blake's later poems is the frustration of human hopes. His sagas of family conflict and cosmic rivalry show humanity in search of fulfilment but thwarted in their search. His two last great illustrated books were *Milton* and *Jerusalem*. *Milton* was written in the aftermath of Felpham and the trial. It is a bewildering poem which centres on a conjoined Blake and Milton. In the course of the poem Blake learns to appreciate the beauty of the natural world, whereas Milton must learn to recant his faith in reason to become truly reconciled to Christ. Like Milton in 'Paradise Lost', Blake is seeking to justify the ways of God to men. But Milton was attempting to justify the renewal of faith in the possibility of revolutionary change in the face of the defeat of the English Revolution. Blake is justifying the rejection of rational demonstration, memory, Bacon, Locke and Newton, in favour of faith and inspiration.

Blake is best known for 'Jerusalem', which is now so familiar as a kind of unofficial national anthem it is hard to imagine it having any radical impact. Those patriots who sing 'Jerusalem' at rugby matches and Tory gatherings imagine it confirms England's special place at the heart of civilisation. England's green and pleasant land is celebrated as specially chosen by Christ.

In fact, 'Jerusalem' carries the opposite message. Blake is demanding to know how anyone could think Christ would choose to walk in England, with its dark satanic mills. It is important to read the first two verses with the question marks firmly in place. Blake is not confirming England's glories – he is questioning them. The poem, bursting with fierce sarcasm in its picture of England's green pastures, ends with devastating lines:

'And did those feet in ancient time
Walk upon England's mountains green?
And was the holy Lamb of God
On England's pleasant pastures seen?

And did the Countenance Divine
Shine forth upon our clouded hills?
And was Jerusalem builded here
Among these dark satanic mills?'

Here there is an emphatic 'no'. No holy Lamb of God would
settle for clouded hills and satanic mills. So revolutionary
action is needed to found a new society in the future:

'Bring me my Bow of burning gold:
Bring me my arrow of desire:
Bring me my spear: O clouds unfold!
Bring me my chariot of fire.
I will not cease my mental fight,
Nor shall my Sword sleep in my hand
Till we have built Jerusalem
In England's green & pleasant Land.'

Jerusalem, the illustrated poem not the song above, is an
ambitious and beautiful poem which blends the Bible with
the history of the ancient British. It involves episodes from
Blake's life, the soldiers and magistrates who accused him,
the reviewers who ridiculed him. The poem celebrates the
God who exists in everyone and the power of the imagination, of which the material world is a mere shadow. Blake

conceives of Jerusalem as a state of mind, not a real city. Los, the character who works at the forge, struggles to achieve his aim, a city of art. Blake refers to contemporary scientific thought about the holistic nature of the human organism and about the power of perception.[72] Blake also constructs images of exploitation, of 'A creation that groans, living by devouring', a system that produces by sucking the life out of the producers.

Jerusalem had around 100 vivid, beautiful etched plates. It was followed by etchings of the Canterbury Pilgrims, illustrations for the Book of Job and Dante's 'Inferno'. These were Blake's last great creative achievements. Blake's health was beginning to fail, although he never stopped receiving friends and visitors and never stopped working on illustrations of Dante and the Bible. Even as late as 1827, when he was very ill, Blake was still conducting his mental fight against hypocrites like Dr Thornton. This good doctor published his New Translation of the Lord's Prayer and Blake responded with undiminished scorn: 'Give us day by day our Real Taxed Substantial Money bought Bread; deliver from the Holy Ghost whatever cannot be Taxed; for all is debts & Tax between Caesar & us & one another'.[73]

Blake had been infamous among his friends for his nervous fears and depressions. But towards the end of his life Blake seemed to find a new peace. He seemed calmer, happier and more contented. Blake told his friend and fellow poet Henry Crabbe Robinson, 'I wish to do nothing for profit. I wish to live for art. I want nothing whatever. I am quite happy'.[74] Shortly before his death, Blake met a pretty, rich young girl at a friend's house. She was surprised when the poor, shabbily dressed Blake said to her, 'May God make this world to you, my child, as beautiful as it has been to me'.[75]

After years of grinding poverty and obscurity, Blake found happiness in his last days. He was working on illustrations for Dante's poetry until days before he died. He was surrounded by young artists who recognised his unique, prophetic abilities and offered him friendship and affection. They recalled that on his deathbed Blake 'burst out singing of the things he saw in heaven'. He told them that he was ready for death, ready 'to get into freedom from all Law of the Members into The Mind in which every one is King & Priest in his own house'. And he was close by his beloved lifelong companion, Catherine.

Blake always believed that an angel had presided over his birth. On his deathbed, the angel was there again, although this time in a more corporeal form – he drew Catherine's portrait and told her, 'You have ever been the angel to me.'

It is an enormous tribute to Blake that, despite all his suffering and disappointments, he died with as much defiance and hatred of authority as he had lived. Blake was buried in Bunhill cemetery, near Old Street station in east London. Today, those visiting Blake's grave find there are always fresh flowers on it, a tribute to the enduring popularity and resonance of the once obscure rebel prophet.

He is always in paradise

Blake was always a dreamer, much to his own frustration: 'I labour incessantly & accomplish not one half of what I intend because my Abstract folly hurries me often away while I am at work, carrying my over Mountains & Valleys which are not real. This I endeavour to prevent & with my whole might chain my feet to the world of Duty & Reality, but in vain!'[76] Catherine Blake told a young acquaintance, 'I have little of Mr Blake's company. He is always in paradise'.[77]

Blake found freedom in his imagination but he also wanted to win freedom in the real world. He wanted to be free from alienation, the state where everything – art, poetry and human beings – were commodities to be bought and sold. He wanted freedom from tyranny, both political and economic. But he could not achieve it. Blake expressed in poetry the impact of the new society on the human spirit. Production was growing beyond the control of any individual and it was regulated only by the forces of the market. This meant relationships between people 'assume in their eyes the fantastic form of a relation between things. In order, therefore, to find an analogy, we must have recourse to the mist-enveloped regions of the religious world'.[78] The reification of the new society mirrored the mystification of religion: Blake encapsulated both.

During Blake's life his craft was destroyed by the new techniques ushered in by the Industrial Revolution. He saw the creative energy and liberation he so desired for humanity brought closer by the revolutionaries of France. As the revolution was overthrown and the monarchy eventually restored he struggled to maintain his faith, just as his great hero John Milton had. He admired Milton precisely because he had been able:

> '...to teach men to despise death and to go on
> In fearless majesty annihilating self, laughing to scorn
> Thy laws and terrors, shaking down thy synagogues
> as webs.'

Milton conjured up images of revolutionary energy and the power of the mind, which were central to Blake's vision 150 years later. Thus Milton's Satan embodies defiance in the face of defeat:

> 'What thought the field be lost:
> All is not lost...
>
> The mind is its own place and in itself
> Can make a heaven of hell, a hell of heaven...
> Better to reign in hell than serve in heaven.'

Blake admired this rebellious spirit. But Milton's heroes achieve their purpose. Blake showed glimpses of liberation, but the potential is always denied. Blake belonged to a class who were the victims of the new society, but lacked the power to decisively challenge it.

Some of his fellow artisans chose activism and agitation instead of daydreams. They believed in their ability to realise liberation in the real world, not only in the world of the imagination. But Blake accused the tyrants and oppressors, and his visionary world has enriched our own. He believed everyone had the capacity to see beyond the world of things:

'To see a World in a Grain of Sand
And a Heaven in a Wild Flower,
Hold Infinity in the palm of your hand
And Eternity in an hour.'

Afterword

Blake's artistic achievement, especially the huge creative effort embodied in the illustrated books, is breathtaking. Yet it was known to only a handful of people during his lifetime. And only a few of them recognised his genius. But with every decade since his death, his audience and his influence has grown. His friends Samuel Palmer and John Linnell promoted his work. Pre-Raphaelite painter Dante Gabriel Rossetti was deeply influenced by Blake's Gothic visions. The first Blake biography, by Alexander Gilchrist, introduced Blake to new admirers and was reprinted four times. In the 20th century artists like Graham Sutherland and Stanley Spencer acknowledged his influence on their work. In 1913 the Tate Gallery staged the first exhibition of Blake's work. In 1947 a touring Blake exhibition visited many European capitals.

In the 1960s a new generation of radical poets and songwriters claimed Blake as their own. They were drawn to him by his hatred of war and oppression, and his disgust with kings, generals and priests.

Allen Ginsberg, the radical poet central to the 'Beat Generation' of post-war artists in the US, was enormously influenced by Blake as poet and visionary. He cited Blake along with Walt Whitman as the poets he most admired. Ginsberg often read Blake's poetry on stage and he set *Songs of Innocence and Experience* to music in 1968, recording an album in 1971. In the sleevenotes, Ginsberg captures the sixties subculture when he says:

'For the soul of the planet is wakening, the time of dissolution of material forms is here, our generation's trapped in imperial satanic cities and nations, and only the prophetic priestly consciousness of the bard Blake, Whitman, or our own new selves – can steady our gaze into the fiery eyes of the tygers of the wrath to come'.[79]

Bob Dylan, who played bass and guitar on some of the songs, freely acknowledges Blake's influence on his writing.

An extremely influential anthology of poetry, *Children of Albion*, published by Penguin in 1969, had Blake's painting 'Glad Day' on the cover. Subtitled *Poetry of the 'Underground' in Britain*, it openly declared for Blake as the tribune of freedom and resistance. Michael Horovitz and Adrian Mitchell, young poets at the time, have remained true to the promise of the anthology and both contributed to Poets Against the War during the war and occupation in Iraq.

Blake was right to think he was creating for eternity. Today, Blake's popularity is still growing around the world. A new generation of anti-war activists, those who hate injustice and oppression, are finding a teacher and an inspiration in William Blake.

Notes

1. Percy Bysshe Shelley used this phrase in a letter to Lord Byron.
2. E P Thompson, *Witness Against the Beast* (CUP, 1994), pxii.
3. D B Pirie, *The Penguin History of Literature Volume 5: The Romantic Period* (Penguin, 1994), p ix.
4. J Bronowski, *William Blake and the Age of Revolution* (Routledge, 1972), p58.
5. Price, op cit, pviii.
6. M Butler, *Romantics, Rebels and Reactionaries* (OUP, 1985), p134.
7. Bronowski, op cit, p5.
8. Pirie, op cit, p7.
9. Bronowski, op cit, p16.
10. G E Bentley, *The Stranger from Paradise: A Biography of William Blake* (Yale, 2001), p5.
11. P Ackroyd, *Blake*, chapter 3 (Sinclair-Stevenson, 1995).
12. Bentley, op cit, p8.
13. Thompson, op cit, p56.

[14] Ibid, p58.

[15] See A L Morton, 'The Everlasting Gospel', in *The Matter of Britain: Essays in a Living Culture* (Lawrence & Wishart, 1966), pp83-122.

[16] Ackroyd, op cit, p26.

[17] Bronowski, op cit, p26.

[18] E Lunn, *Marxism and Modernism* (Verso, 1985), p15.

[19] Ibid, p16.

[20] Bronowski, op cit, p23.

[21] Ackroyd, op cit, p72.

[22] Bronowski, op cit, p59.

[23] P Linebaugh, *The London Hanged: Crime and Civil Society in the Eighteenth Century* (Allen Lane, 1991), p330.

[24] Bentley, op cit, p56.

[25] Bronowski, op cit, p61.

[26] D V Erdman, *Blake: Prophet Against Empire* (Dover, 1991), p11.

[27] Bentley, op cit, p28.

[28] Ibid, p106.

[29] M Butler, *Tate Exhibition Guide* (Tate, 2000), p16.

[30] Ackroyd, op cit, p87.

[31] K Raine, *William Blake* (Thames and Hudson, 1970), chapter 2.

[32] Bentley, op cit, p112.

[33] Ibid, p113.

[34] Butler, *Tate Exhibition Guide*, op cit, p153.

[35] Bentley, op cit, p196.

[36] Bronowski, op cit, p66.

[37] B Ollman, *Alienation: Marx's Conception of Man in*

Capitalist Society (CUP, 1971), p137.

[38]   Thompson, op cit, p63.

[39]   P Foot, 'A Passionate Prophet of Liberation', *International Socialism* 71, Summer 1996.

[40]   Bentley, op cit, p5.

[41]   Butler, *Tate Exhibition Guide*, op cit, p16.

[42]   Bentley, op cit, p133.

[43]   Ackroyd, op cit, p130.

[44]   E J Hobsbawm, *Age of Revolution* (Weidenfeld and Nicolson, 1962), p103.

[45]   Thompson, op cit, p7.

[46]   Given the population was around one million at the time this was their 15 February 2003, when two million marched in London against Bush and Blair's war on Iraq.

[47]   Bronowski, op cit, p74.

[48]   Bentley, op cit, p113.

[49]   Ackroyd, op cit, p160.

[50]   Raine, op cit, p56.

[51]   Erdman, op cit, p190.

[52]   Bentley, op cit, p135.

[53]   Ackroyd, op cit, p126.

[54]   Thompson, op cit, p179.

[55]   Butler, *Tate Exhibition Guide*, op cit, p19.

[56]   Lunn, op cit, p3.

[57]   E P Thompson, *The Making of the English Working Class* (Gollancz, 1965), p145.

[58]   Bentley, op cit, p203.

[59]   Bronowski, op cit, p111.

[60] Ibid, p108.

[61] Bentley, op cit, p263.

[62] Ackroyd, op cit, p251.

[63] Bentley, op cit, p278.

[64] Ibid, p282.

[65] P Foot, op cit.

[66] R Holmes, *Coleridge: Early Visions* (HarperCollins, 1998), p33.

[67] Lord Byron wrote a poem condemning the introduction of the death penalty.

[68] Bronowski, op cit, p174.

[69] Holmes, op cit, p242.

[70] Ackroyd, op cit, p323; and Bentley, op cit, p349.

[71] Bentley, op cit, p356.

[72] See for example, David Hartley's *Observations on Man, his Fame, his Duties, his Expectations* (1749).

[73] Bronowski, op cit, p116.

[74] Ackroyd, op cit, p342.

[75] Bentley, op cit, p364.

[76] Ibid, p270.

[77] Ackroyd, op cit, p295.

[78] Lunn, op cit, p16.

[79] A Ginsberg, *Deliberate Prose: Selected Writings 1952-1995* (HarperCollins, 2000), p279.